Paleo Slow Cooker

Top 65+ Easy and Delicious Paleo Slow Cooker Recipes for Weight Loss and Nutritious Meals

By

NANCY KELSEY

NANCY KELSEY

ISBN-13: 978-1519406156
ISBN-10: 1519406150

Disclaimer

All the material contained in this book is provided for educational and informational purposes only. No responsibility can be taken for any results or outcomes resulting from the use of this material.

While every attempt has been made to provide information that is both accurate and effective, the author does not assume any responsibility for the accuracy or use/misuse of this information.

Contents

Roast Stew Paleo

Slow Cooker Paleo Meatballs

Paleo Crockpot Shredded Beef

Hearty Crock Pot Chili Stew

5-Spice Slow-Cooker Pork Ribs

Easy Barbecue Slow Cooker Ribs

Slow Cooker Pulled Pork

Slow Cooker Chinese Spare Ribs

Easy Slow Cooker Kalua Pork

Slow Cooker Baby Back Ribs + Paleo BBQ Sauce

Slow Cooker Balsamic Pulled Pork With Polenta

Easy Slow Cooked

Slow Cooker Beef Rendang

Beef Bone Broth

Paleo Slow Cooker Breakfast Casserole

Crock Pot Beef Stew

Slow Cooker Spicy Indian Beef Roast

Picadillo Paleo

Meaty Paleo Chili

Slow Cooker Pot Roast

Paleo Slow Cooker Shin Beef

Slow Cooker Pork Stew W Oyster Mushrooms

Slow Cooker Chicken Yellow Curry Soup

Crockpot Stuffed Chicken Breasts

Lemon & Artichoke Slow Cooker Chicken

Easy Crock Pot Roasted Chicken w/ Lemon Parsley Butter

Crock-Pot Kalua Chicken Tacos With Chili Lime Mango Salsa

Slow Cooked Gizzard Recipe

Slow Cooker Lemon Chicken Thighs

Slow Cooker Basic Chicken Stock

Crockpot Chicken Cacciatore

Crock Pot Chicken Stock

Paleo Chicken Tortilla Soup Recipe

Slow Cooker Paleo Chicken Soup Recipe

Crockpot Chicken Stock

Homemade Chicken Variation)

Slow Cooker Mexican Chicken Soup

Slow Cooker Chocolate Chicken Mole

Slow Cooker Coconut Curried Chicken

Balsamic Pot Roast Gravy with Roasted Garlic Mash.

Easy Paleo Pot

Crockpot Pork Roast

Pot Roast Soup

Why Paleo?

In Brief: It's the best! A Paleo diet can alter your life..

Many do not have the knowledge that some fundamental alterations in your diet plan can help you achieve a health mind and body, and it will also help you to lose the excess flab and to get fit.

The Primal or Paleo lifestyle and its origins can be traced back to a few decades, but it got immense popularity after the start of this millennium.

Paleo the term comes from Paleolithic age and it has been developed keeping in mind, i.e. the diet our ancestors used to follow before the advent of farming (pulses and grains in particular).

This diet has healed many, and there is an endless stream of success stories from real people. People who were diagnosed with obesity, depression, diabetes, skin problems like eczema and have fought it successfully with Paleo diet and lifestyle. There are many others, who have started this diet plan for a better life.

There's abundant information about it, and there are a lot of experts who have shared their knowledge on the internet and also through books.

But, why Swiss Paleo, when there is so much data at

your disposal?

As soon as I got to know about Paleo, about a couple months back, I wanted to use it that instance. However, whilst living over at Switzerland, I always ended up being disappointed. That's because, first of all I did not know where to buy some of the ingredients, and I did know the German translations for them.

But thankfully, I contacted my friend and the Paleo Guru Lisa, who helped me and made me understand about the ingredients. It took me 30 full days to understand. But, the trail did work out!

I also understood that if people in Germany, Austria and Switzerland tried buying Paleo, they can endure some difficulties, as most of them do not have Lisa by their sides.

But, with this, the whole concept of Paleo was born out.

Swiss Paleo would be your electronic data base on how to shift your diet and your subsequent lifestyle whilst staying in the German speaking world. And, we wish that, in the near future, if possible, we'll be able to provide classes right at Zurich too.

Also, besides altering your diet, the Paleo based life

also concerns with exercise regimes. Of course, this does not mean will run your legs out like the 80s!

We'll just provide you with some knowhow and give your some data—like details and videos—about what you should do at home. Instructions for these will be given be Fitness Guru, Julie.

So, do not be shy to make continuous visits to the site and see out all our new updates and changes. Also do remember to check out all our new recipes, shopping guides, pantry items, news, fitness videos and various other articles on our very own Paleo tour.

15 Fundamental points about Paleo Diet

➤ The fat content should be high and carbohydrate content should be medium or less than that. There should be enough animal protein, the quantity should be medium. The serving size and calorific values need not be maintained.

➤ Have as much saturated fats as you want. In a Paleo diet there are no restrictions over butter, coconut oil, clarified butter. For a better health you can also try beef tallow, duck fat and lard. For oils that can only be used in salads, you can try out olive oil, avocado oil, and macadamia oil.

➢ Animal protein is essential for your body and builds muscles. Like red meat, pork, eggs, poultry, organs of animals-liver , heart, kidney), fish. You should also have fat that comes along with animal protein; you can cook stocks, stews and broth with these animal proteins. Large portions or quantities are advised.

➢ Have a lot of fresh or refrigerated veggies, it could be cooked or uncooked. These starchy foods like sweet potatoes or yam, which provide us with non-toxic carbs.

➢ Take fruits and nuts- Eat low sugar fruits and fruits that have a lot of antioxidants like berries, and rich in omega -3 like nuts, and you can eat macadamia nuts which is low in polyunsaturated fat. Do not consume nuts and fruits if you have stomach problems, autoimmune disease or if you are in a diet plan to reduce your weight.

➢ Take grass fed or meat that have been raised on nearby farmland, which have been raised keeping in mind environmental factors. Otherwise take small amounts of meat and other than that you can have coconut oils, butter and clarified butter. And you can also have local veggies and fruits, which vary according to seasons.

- Do not have cereal in the diet plan. And also cut grains, legumes. Rye, barley, oats, corn, brown rice, soy, peanuts, navy beans and black-eyed peas are included but are not limited to this.

- Oils- you can have avocado and olive oil, but only with salads. Do not have vegetable, hydrogenated oils or partially hydrogenated oils like maragarine, soybean oil, corn oil, peanut oil, canola oil, sunflower oil etc.

- Take sugar cautiously and cut down on soft drinks, sweets, juices, and any packaged food items. Eat fresh produce, like veggies, meat ,fish and not canned items

- You can have butter and cream as much as you want but cut down on all other dairy or milk products, if you want to have dairy or milk products have it raw milk products and fermented products.

- The thumb rule of eating three square meals a day is not applicable here, eat whenever you are hungry and do not be stressed or tensed, if a meal is skipped in a day. It could also be more than one meal.

- Need to have a proper rest. Like sleeping for eight hours in the night is mandatory. And go to bed early, and avoid stressors like alcohol, coffee and other external factors or stressors. And in the morning wake up without an alarm, so that the biological clock is set.

➢ Exercise or train your body to do physical work, but do not over do it, at any point of time. Do it around four times a week. Take rest if you get tired, and do small but effective and intense running or sprinting sessions. It would better than long cardio sessions.

➢ Have some sources from where vitamin D and probiotics, magnesium, iodine and Vitamin K2 can be extracted. Seaweeds are a good source of iodine. Have a supplemental source of procuring these minerals and vitamins.

➢ Go out have fun, be adventurous, travel, play outdoor sports, chill, gain knowledge, have fun with people and friends and do not forget to spread happiness and enjoy your life!

Crockpot Pulled Pork Chili

- Prep Time :10 Mins
- Cook Time : 10 Hours
- Total Time : 10 Hours 10 Mins
- Serves: 6-8

Ingredients

- 2 Pound Pork Roast
- 3 Garlic Cloves, Peeled
- ½ Cup Hot Sauce
- 3 Tablespoons Smoked Paprika
- 2 Tablespoons Garlic Powder
- 2 Tablespoon Chili Powder
- 1 Tablespoon Cumin
- 2 Teaspoons Cayenne Pepper
- 1 Heaping Tablespoon Red Pepper Flakes
- Lots Of Salt
- 2 Yellow Onions, Diced
- 1 Red Bell Pepper, Diced
- 1 Yellow Bell Pepper, Diced
- 2 (14) Ounce Cans Of Fire Roasted Tomatoes
- 1 (14) Ounce Can Of Tomato Sauce
- Avocado, Sliced (To Garnish)
- Green Onions, Diced (To Garnish)

How to make it:

1. Take a crock pot or slow cooking pot and put the roasted pork in it.

2. Make some holes in the pork roast with a sharp tool like a knife and add cloves of garlic after peeling the skin of the garlic.
3. To spice it up, put garlic powder, cumin, cayenne, paprika & some pepper flakes.
4. Before that, do not forget to add the hot or spicy sauce on it.
5. Now lay over the tomatoes, minced onions, pepper and tomato sauce over the pork. Use perfectly cut slices of green onions & avocado to embellish the dish.
6. And before embellishing it, you have to cook it for eight to ten hours by setting the heat to low.

****

Slow Cooker Paleo BBQ Brisket Recipe

- Prep Time : 5 Mins
- Total Time : 10 Hours 5 Mins
- Serves: 6 Servings :

Ingredients

- 3 Lb Brisket
- 10-12 Oz (300g) Tomato Paste
- 1 Cup (250ml) Water
- 1 Tablespoon Salt
- 2 Tablespoons Tamari Sauce (Or Coconut Aminos)
- 3 Tablespoons Raw Honey
- 2 Tablespoons Apple Cider Vinegar

- ½ Tablespoon Cinnamon Powder

How to make it

1. Take the constituents in a crock pot and blend them together.
2. Put the brisket in the crockpot and pour the sauce over it.
3. Heat it for ten to twelve hours at a low temperature.
4. Before eating, you should first bring out the brisket from the crockpot with some BBQ sauce.
5. And put the shredded brisket and sauce on the stove for a few minutes, less than five minutes would be proper.
6. The heat will lessen the sauce and a pinch of salt to make it better.

****

Paleo Slow Cooker Oxtail Stew Recipe

- Prep Time: 5 Mins
- Cook Time : 10 Hours 15 Mins
- Total Time : 10 Hours 20 Mins
- Serves: 4 Servings

Ingredients

- 4 Lb Oxtail (Chopped Into Segments - Get Your Butcher To Do This If Possible)

- 1-2 Cups Of Water (To Fill Up Half The Crockpot/Slowcooker)
- 2 14oz (400g) Cans Of Diced Tomatoes (Or 10 Fresh Tomatoes, Diced)
- 10 Cloves Garlic, Crushed
- 4 Teaspoons Paprika (Add More If Preferred)
- 2 Tablespoons Italian Seasoning (Optional - Great Instead Of Paprika E.G., F You Don't Like Any Heat In Your Stew)
- Dash Of Chili Powder (Optional)
- Salt To Taste

How to make it

1. At first you should take a crockpot, and put some water in it.
2. Put the oxtail into the water and heat it for around ten hours. The setting for the heat should be low.
3. When the meat is soft and tender, it's ready to be added to the stew.
4. The stew could be made in a stewpot or saucepan where tomatoes, spices and garlic is combined with the oxtail.
5. Cook it for under quarter of an hour, and your oxtail stew is ready to be served.
6. Do not forget to put some salt in it.

- **************

Homemade Thai Chicken Broth

- Prep Time : 5 Mins
- Total Time : 8 Hours 5 Mins
- Serves: 10+ Servings

Ingredients

- 1 Whole Chicken
- 1 Stalk Of Lemongrass, Cut Into Large Chunks
- 20 Fresh Basil Leaves (10 For The Slow Cooker, And 10 For Garnish)
- 5 Thick Slices Of Fresh Ginger
- 1 Lime
- 1 Tablespoon Salt
- Additional Salt To Taste

How to make it

1. Begin with a slow cooker or crockpot and put lemongrass, ten basil leaves, salt, ginger and the before all that put the chicken in the crock pot.
2. Put water in the crock pot and heat it for less than 10 hours.
3. Take a small bowl and use a ladle or dipper and put the blended broth into the bowl and decorate it with basil leaves.

4. And also put some salt and limejuice to make it taste better.
5. And your Thai chicken broth is ready to be consumed.

******

Slow Cooker Paleo Jerk Chicken

- Prep Time 10 Mins
- Total Time5 Hours 10 Mins
- Serves: 4 Servings

Ingredients

- 5 Drumsticks And 5 Wings (Or You Can Use A Whole Chicken Or 5 Chicken Breasts)
- 4 Teaspoons Of Salt
- 4 Teaspoons Of Paprika
- 1 Teaspoons Of Cayenne Pepper
- 2 Teaspoons Of Onion Powder
- 2 Teaspoons Of Thyme
- 2 Teaspoons Of White Pepper
- 2 Teaspoons Of Garlic Powder
- 1 Teaspoons Of Black Pepper

How to make it:-

1. Take all the spices and blend it in a container.

2. To make it non-spicy, just put onion powder in the place of cayenne pepper.
3. Use clean water to cleanse the chicken properly and apply the blend on to the chicken in the container.
4. The chicken would be little bit hot or spicy because of the paprika present in the spices.
5. Putting the blend inside the skin of the chicken would make it better.
6. For this purpose chicken drumsticks and wings are better .
7. As it is easier to place the blend in the wings and the drumstick.
8. Now put the chicken pieces inside the crock pot. Cook it for five or six hours and the heat should be fixed at 325 Degrees Fahrenheit, or at medium or low setting.
9. The meat is done when it gets separated. When that happens, your Paleo Jerk Chicken is ready to be served; you can serve it with bone or without it.

******

Slow Cooker Bacon & Chicken

- Serves: 4 Servings

Ingredients

- 5 Chicken Breasts

- 10 Slices Of Bacon
- 2 Tablespoons Thyme (Dried)
- 1 Tablespoon Oregano (Dried)
- 1 Tablespoon Rosemary (Dried)
- 5 Tablespoons Olive Oil (2 Tablespoons For The Slow Cooker And 3 Tablespoons After Cooking)
- 1 Tablespoon Salt

How to make it

1. First take a crock pot and blend all the items.
2. The heat should be set to low. Heat it for around eight hours.
3. When it's done, you need to put around three tablespoons of olive oil in the meat but before that the meat has to be cut into pieces or has to be shredded perfectly.
4. Your slow cooker bacon is ready to be enjoyed!

******

Paleo Ropa Vieja Recipe

- Prep Time20 Mins
- Total Time20 Mins
- Serves: 6-8 Servings

Ingredients

- 3lb Flank Steak
- 2 Tablespoons Coconut Oil (For Pan Searing)
- ¼ Cup Olive Oil
- 1 Tablespoon White Wine Vinegar
- 2 Tablespoons Of Sea Salt
- ¼ Cup Cilantro, Finely Chopped
- ¼ Cup Parsley, Finely Chopped
- 2 Cloves Garlic, Crushed
- 2 (6oz) Cans Tomato Paste
- 3 Peppers, Sliced
- 1 Tablespoon Onion Flakes (Or Onion Powder)
- 1 Tablespoon Garlic Powder
- 1 Tablespoon Oregano
- 1 Tablespoon Cumin Powder

How to make it:-

1. First take the flank steak or a flat cut steak and use a sharp tool to divide into two inch thick pieces.
2. Then take a big fillet or greased up frying pan and put a tablespoon of coconut oil in it and turn the heat unto high.
3. Take the cut steak pieces (take only half at first) and sear it in the pan for around two-two three minutes, when one side is over, heat the other side.
4. And after it is finished, do the same thing with the rest of the pieces.

5. Now take all the items in a crockpot with the seared meat. Blend it well, if need be combine everything with your hands.
6. Now heat up the crockpot, set it to low and continue heating it for six hours or so with the mix.
7. After it's over the meat has to be shredded or cut up into small fragments and blend everything well.
8. It's now ready to be served and enjoyed!

******

Slow Cooked Corned Beef Brisket and Roasted Cabbage

Ingredients:-

Slow Cooked Corned Beef Brisket

- 2½ Lb Corned Beef Brisket
- ½ Medium Onion
- 1 Carrot
- 1 Celery Stalk
- 1 Cup Chicken Or Beef Stock

Roasted Cabbage

- 1 Head Of Green Cabbage
- 1 Tablespoon Avocado Oil
- Salt And Pepper To Taste

How to make it

Slow Cooked Corned Beef Brisket

1. Take a slow cooker or crockpot and take diced onions, celery and carrot and put it on the base of the cooker.
2. Then put the corned beef on the vegetables and before that add the chicken stock or beef stock over the vegetables-celery, carrot and onions.
3. Heat the cooker for eight hours or less, the minimum time should be six hours.
4. And while heating it remember to put a lid over the cooker.

Roasted Cabbage

1. Set the oven temperature at 450 Degrees Fahrenheit.
2. Take a baking sheet and over it the cabbage which has been cut into eight pieces.
3. Use avocado oil, pepper and some salt over the sides.
4. Then take the pieces of cabbage in the oven for less than half an hour and continue to move it till the sides become brown and crunchy.
5. When it has reached this stage your cabbage roast is done and it is ready to be eaten.

Slow Cooker Lemongrass Coconut Chicken Drumsticks

Ingredients:-

- 10 Drumsticks, Skin Removed
- 1 Thick Stalk Fresh Lemongrass, Papery Outer Skins And Rough Bottom Removed, Trimmed To The Bottom 5 Inches
- 4 Cloves Garlic, Minced
- 1 Thumb-Size Piece Of Ginger, Microplaned
- 1 Cup Coconut Milk
- 2 Tablespoons red Boat Fish Sauce
- 3 Tablespoons Coconut Aminos
- 1 Teaspoon Five Spice Powder
- 1 Large Onion, Thinly Sliced
- ¼ Cup Fresh Cilantro, Chopped
- Kosher Salt
- Freshly Ground Pepper

How to make it

1. Take a pot or bowl where you have to make a soft and saucy blend with a blender.
2. And the blend or sauce would be made from lemongrass, ginger, garlic, coconut milk, fish sauce, coconut and mixed spices.
3. Now take another container where you have to put all the drumsticks and combine it with pepper and salt.
4. And blend it well with the marinade.

5. Put diced onions at the base of the crockpot and top it with the marinade and drumsticks.
6. The temperature should be set to low and heat it for around four to five hours.
7. Sprinkle some fish sauce, some black pepper and also add a little bit of salt over it after it has been cooked.
8. Finally, embellish it with some scallions or cilantro.

Slow Cooker Beef Stew with Cranberries and Rosemary

Ingredients:-

- 2 lbs. beef stew meat (cut into same size pieces)
- 2 bunches of radishes (scrubbed and trimmed, but left whole)
- 1 lb. celery root (peeled & cut into 1 inch cubes)
- 1 lb. carrots (peeled and thickly sliced)
- 3 cups bone broth
- 1 teaspoon salt (less if your broth is salted)
- 1/2 tsp. black pepper (optional – omit for AIP)
- 2 large onions (peeled whole)
- 2 large cloves garlic (peeled whole)
- 2 branches fresh rosemary
- 8 oz. bag of frozen cranberries (save these for the final step in the recipe)

How to make it

1. Start with a crockpot and put beef, radishes, carrots, celery root, bone broth, salt and pepper.
2. Combine it properly.
3. Put two onions, and then put two cloves of garlic over the onions.
4. At last put the rosemary branches over everything and cook it for around eight hours while setting the temperature to low.
5. When it is done, take the onions and garlic cloves out and put in a mixer blender, and use a dipper or ladle to take out some broth, puree over the onions and the garlic.
6. After it has been blended, shift everything to the slow cooker and put frozen cranberries and mix it well.
7. Then put the lid and heat for another half an hour, while setting the temperature to low.
8. Salt can be adjusted according to taste.
9. Your stew is ready to be savored!

Slow Cooker Beef Stroganoff

Ingredients:-

- 2 lbs. beef stew meat
- 2 tsp. salt

- 1/2 tsp. pepper
- 1 tsp. garlic powder
- 2 tsp. paprika
- 1 tsp. thyme
- 1 tsp. onion powder
- 8 oz. sliced mushrooms
- 1/2 onion, sliced
- 1/3 c. coconut cream (scooped from the top of a refrigerated can of coconut milk)
- 2 tsp. red wine vinegar

How to make it

1. Begin with a small pot or bowl where you have to combine all the spices.
2. Then atke another large bowl or pot where the meat has to be kept.
3. Drizzle the meat with the spies. Blend everything properly with your hand.
4. Then put the thinly cut mushrooms and onions in a bowl in crockpot.
5. Then put the prepared beef in the crockpot.
6. Then you have to heat it for four and half hours. Remember to close the lid.
7. If the meat becomes soft then it is ready to be taken out.
8. Then put the coconut cream, vinegar, salt or pepper in the crockpot and blend it properly with a spoon.
9. Heat it without the cover for nearly an hour or so. Your dish is now ready to be served!

<u>Crockpot Thai Beef Stew</u>

- SERVES: 6-8
- PREP TIME:20mins
- COOK TIME:300-480 mins
- TOTAL TIME: 320 mins

<u>Ingredients:-</u>

- 2 tablespoons coconut oil, divided
- 3 pounds beef stew meat, trimmed of fat
- 1 medium yellow onion, thinly sliced
- 2 cloves garlic, minced
- 2 teaspoons peeled and minced fresh ginger
- 1 (13.5-ounce) can full-fat coconut milk
- 1/3 cup tomato paste
- 1/2 cup Thai red curry paste
- 2 tablespoons fish sauce
- 2 teaspoons fresh lime juice
- 2 teaspoons sea salt
- 2 cups broccoli florets
- 2 cups julienned carrots
- 1 cup peeled and julienned jicama*
- fresh cilantro, for garnish

<u>How to make it:-</u>

1. First take a skillet or frying pan and heat one tablespoon of coconut oil in it.
2. Set the temperature to medium high and put the meat, but not altogether.

3. Then take a slotted spoon for transferring batch of browned meat on the skillet.
4. Clean the bottom of the skillet for even cooking.
5. When it is done, clean the skillet and put one tablespoon of coconut oil, and fry onion, garlic, and ginger over medium heat for around five minutes.
6. Then put the coconut milk and blend it constantly, so that the excess small brown pieces or bits, reach the bottom.
7. Then pour the paste of tomato, curry, fish sauce lime juice and salt and put the mix on the beef, in the crockpot.
8. Heat it for five hours when the temperature is set to high and for eight hours when it's set to low. Embellish it with cilantro while serving it.

****

Slow Cooker Squeaky Clean Boeuf Bourgignon

• Yield: Serves 4 to 6

Ingredients:-

- 900g (2lbs) grass-fed beef stew meat
- 1 large onion, chopped
- 2 cloves garlic, chopped
- 2 large carrots, peeled and sliced
- 1 small (1½ cups) turnip, peeled and diced

- 2-3 sprigs fresh rosemary, whole
- 2 Bay leaves
- 1 tsp Himalayan salt
- 1 tsp freshly cracked black pepper
- 2 tbsp Dijon mustard
- 2 cups bone broth
- 1/4 cup red wine vinegar
- 227g (1/2lb) mushrooms, sliced
- 2 tbsp tapioca starch
- 2 tbsp water

How To Make It:-

1. The meat has to be dried first and put pepper and salt over it, liberally.
2. Take a skillet or a frying pan to melt ghee,lard or to fry coconut oil.
3. Set the temperature to high.
4. Then put the meat over the pan and there should be some space between the pieces.
5. Heat it till the point it changes its color to brown.
6. Take the meat pieces out in a bowl or pot so that the juices get drained.
7. And in the pan put some more oil if needed and fry the onion and garlic.
8. Blend it constantly. Put the broth, red wine vinegar, Dijon mustard and heat it.
9. Then again transfer the meat and juices over the skillet.
10. Then take all the things and shift it to a crockpot and put carrots, turnip, mushrooms, rosemary and bay leaves.

11. Heat it for eight hours by setting the temperature to low and for six hours by setting the temperature to high.
12. When it is cooked fully use a dipper to put it on a pot or saucepan, and boil it. And in another container, combine tapioca and water and then put it in the liquid.
13. Then take the sauce onto the crockpot and blend it till it gets smooth.
14. Top it with bay leaves and rosemary sprigs before serving it.

Slow-Cooker Beef Brisket With Bourbon BBQ Sauce

Ingredients

- 1 Batch Bourbon Spiked BBQ Sauce
- 1 3 To 4 Lb Beef Brisket
- 1 Onion, Sliced
- Salt, Pepper, Granulated Garlic
- 1 Tbs Coconut Oil, To Sear The Brisket

How to make it:-

1. At first prepare a Bourbon spiked BBQ sauce.
2. Then take a big skillet or deep frying pan, and heat some coconut oil in it.

3. Then put some salt, pepper, granulated garlic over the brisket.
4. Fry the brisket for 2 mins, flip the sides, till the meat has a good brown crust.
5. After that put some onions in the crockpot and put the fried brisket over that.
6. Then put the BBQ sauce over them. Blend them properly.
7. Then cover the slow cooker and heat for six to eight hours when the temperature is set to low.
8. When it is finished, the meat would be quite soft.
9. Before serving it, the beef has to be shredded into pieces, with a knife or a fork.

Roast Stew Paleo

- Prep time: 10 mins
- Cook time: 7 hours
- Total time: 7 hours 10 mins

Ingredients

- ½ pound of organic uncured bacon, in strips
- 2 to 3 pound grass-fed and -finished chuck roast
- 2 large organic red onions, peeled and cut in slices
- 1 clove organic garlic, peeled and smashed
- 1 small organic green or Savoy cabbage
- Celtic sea salt

- Fresh ground black pepper to taste
- 1 sprig fresh organic thyme
- 1 cup of homemade beef bone broth

How to make it:-

1. Start with a crockpot and put bacon pieces or slices in the crockpot.
2. Put some onion pieces and garlic; add the chuck roast, cabbage pieces, broth, thyme and some sea salt with generous amount of ground black pepper.
3. Heat the crockpot fro seven hours and set the temperature to low.
4. Now you can enjoy your stew in small bowls.

Slow Cooker Paleo Meatballs

Ingredients:-

- 3lbs Ground Beef
- 1/4 cup finely cut spinach
- 2 tbls finely chopped onion
- 1 tsp garlic salt
- salt and pepper
- oil
- favorite pasta sauce

How to make it:-

1. At first start with a mixing bowl or container and mix the spinach, onions, salt, garlic salt, salt and pepper with ground beef.
2. Blend it well. Then make a few meatballs, one or two inches in size.
3. Put them aside.
4. And take a skillet or frying pan and heat some oil in it.
5. Put the meatballs in the skillet and make it brown. Then put it in the crockpot and put some sauce over it.
6. Heat it for a four to five hours while setting the temperature to low.

Paleo Crockpot Shredded Beef

- Prep time: 5 mins
- Total time: 5 hours 5 mins

Ingredients:-

- 3.5 lb chuck / pot roast
- ¼ cup preferred stock
- ½ tsp salt
- 1 tsp black pepper
- ½ tblsp oregano
- ½ tsp cumin
- ¼ tspanchochile
- ¼ tsp paprika

- ⅛ tsp cinnamon
- ½ tsp garlic
- 2 tblsp tomato paste

For the sauce:

- ¾ cup skimmed stock / meat juices (see below)
- ¼ onion, diced
- 2 cloves garlic
- 1 jalapeno, diced
- ¼ tsp salt
- ¼ tsp cumin
- ¼ tsp black pepper
- ¼ tspanchochile
- ½ cup salsa
- ½ chopped tomatoes or sauce

How to make it :-

Shredded beef:-

1. Take a slow cooker to begin with and stock at the bottom and put some tomato paste.
2. Place the chuck or pot roast in the slow cooker. And drizzle the spices over it and heat it for five hours.
3. Then take the meat out of the slow cooker and shred the meat with forks or knife.
4. Then we have to separate the fat layer or solid layer from the refrigerated meat juices and use only the liquid part.

Sauce:

1. Take the meat juices and heat it on a stove and put jalapeno, garlic and onions and keep it simmered to make it soft and to let the excess liquid to get evaporated.
2. Do this for five minutes.
3. Apply salsa and tomato over it, then take it from the heat and stir it till, the point it gets mixed properly.
4. Then pour it over the meat.

Hearty Crock Pot Chili Stew

- Prep time20 mins
- Cook time5 hours
- Total time5 hours 20 mins
- Serves: 12

Ingredients

- 1 lb Ground Beef
- 1 lb Cubed Beef Stew Meat
- 1 28 ounce Can Tomato Puree or Tomato Sauce (one with tomatoes as only ingredient)
- 2 Cups Organic GF Beef Broth or homemade.
- ½ cup pureed pumpkin, or can use ½ cup canned pumpkin puree for thickening.
- 2 Cups Sliced Mushrooms
- 1 Medium Zucchini Squash, chopped

- 1 Medium Onion, Minced
- 6 Cloves Garlic, Minced
- 3 Tbsp Chili Powder
- 1 Tbsp Cumin
- 1 Tsp Garlic Powder
- 2 Tbsp coconut oil or olive oil

How to make it :-

1. First take a big skillet or pan and heat the beef till it gets brown.
2. Then use a crockpot and set the temperature to high.
3. Put tomato puree, beef broth, pumpkin puree, two tablespoon of chili powder, ne teaspoon of garlic powder and one tablespoon of cumin to crock pot and blend it well.
4. Then take one tablespoon of olive oil into the skillet and fry the onions, minced garlic, mushrooms and zucchini squash.
5. Fry till the vegetables become soft.
6. Then put all the vegetable in the slow cooker. In the skillet fry one tablespoon of chili powder, beef stew meat in one tablespoon of olive or coconut oil.
7. Fry till the point the beef becomes brown. Then put the beef stew meat in the slow cooker.
8. Put the lid over it and cook for two to five hours if the temperature is set to low or two hours if it's set to high.

5-Spice Slow-Cooker Pork Ribs

- Prep 2 min.
- Cook 6-12 hours in slow cooker

Ingredients:-

- 3-4 pounds baby back or St. Louis pork ribs
- salt and ground black pepper
- 2 teaspoons Chinese five-spice powder
- 3/4 teaspoon coarse (granulated) garlic powde
- 1 fresh jalapeño, cut into rings
- 2 tablespoons rice vinegar
- 2 tablespoons coconut aminos or homemade substitute
- 1 tablespoon tomato paste

How to make it:

1. Take the ribs and cut into thin pieces.
2. Then place the ribs on a plain surface and put some salt and pepper in it.
3. Then take a small bowl or container and combine Chinese five spices, garlic powder and properly apply it on the meat.
4. Then put the jalapeno on the base of the crockpot and pour rice vinegar, coconut aminos, and tomato paste over it. Blend until the tomato paste has been combined with other items.

5. The put the ribs vertically, and you can put a roasting rack in the crockpot to stop the meat from lying down.
6. Heat for eight to ten hours when the temperature is set to low or for six hours if the temperature is set to high.
7. It is done, when the ribs become soft and then it is time to take it out of the cooker.
8. Put the liquid into a heat- proof container and refrigerate it, till the time the fat separates.
9. Take out the fat and boil the liquid for a few minutes. To make the ribs crunchy, heat it at 400 Degrees Fahrenheit.

Easy Barbecue Slow Cooker Ribs

Ingredients:-

- 2 Racks Of Pork Ribs, Cut In Half For 4 Total Segments (Approximately 6-7 Lb Total)
- 1/2 Tbspancho Chili Pepper Powder
- 1/2 Tbsp Chipotle Chili Pepper Powder
- 1/4 Tsp Cinnamon
- 1/4 Tsp Cumin
- Salt And Pepper, To Taste
- 1 Whole White Onion, Sliced
- 6 Cloves Garlic, Crushed
- 1 Tbsp Of Gheeor Fat Of Choice

- 2 C Brian's Barbecue Sauce

How to make it:

1. Switch on the oven and heat it to 400 Degrees Fahrenheit.
2. Take the thin layer out of the lower side of the ribs; it would be like a membrane.
3. Then divide or cut them into two equal pieces. Drizzle some ancho chili pepper, chili pepper, chipotle, cinnamon, cumin and mashed garlic.
4. Also add some pepper and salt.
5. Take a baking sheet and keep it on it and heat it in the oven for fifteen mins.
6. Simultaneously, cut the onions and peel and mash the garlic. Put some ghee, cloves of garlic, and onions in the crockpot.
7. Apply BBQ sauce over the ribs., and put any of the excess sauce on the stacked ribs in the crockpot.
8. Put a lid over the crock pot and heat for six hours and at med-low temperature.
9. After it has been cooked, take it out of the crockpot and keep it aside for the flavors to sink in, then divide it into pieces, or slices.
10. Serve it with additional BBQ sauce if you like.

Slow Cooker Pulled Pork

- Yield: 12 servings

Ingredients:-

For the pulled pork:-

- 3lb boneless pork shoulder (aka. Boston Butt)
- 1 tsp onion powder
- 1 tsp garlic powder
- 1 tsp kosher salt
- 1/2 tsp black pepper
- 1/2 tsp paprika
- 1/2 tsp ground allspice
- 1/2 tsp celery salt
- 1/8 tsp ground cloves
- 1/2 tsp mustard powder
- 1/2 cup water

For the BBQ sauce:-

- 1/2 tsp ground allspice
- 1/4 cup prepared yellow mustard
- 2 tsp hot sauce (I used Frank's Red Hot)
- 3 Tbsp apple cider vinegar
- 3 Tbsp low sugar ketchup
- 4 Tbsp granulated sugar substitute
- 1/2 tsp xanthan gum

How to make it

1. Pulled pork-Take a small bowl or mixing pot and blend all the powdered-garlic, onion, mustard in it.
2. Then also put salt, pepper, paprika, celery salt, cloves and all spices.
3. Blend it properly.
4. Apply the blend over the pork.
5. Then take a slow cooker and put water in it.
6. Then put the readied pork in it.
7. Close the lid and heat for five hours while setting the temperature to high.
8. Heat it till the point it becomes soft and it gets separated.
9. Then take it out, leave some of the juices for later use.
10. And use a knife or a couple of forks for shredding the meat into pieces.

A. Sauce-begin with separating the solid from above the liquid.
B. Then put the items for making the sauce in the slow cooker and stir or blend constantly. And heat it for ten minutes while setting the temperature to high. It's ready to be served hot, when becomes slightly thick.
C. While serving put the meat over the sauce and combine it properly. Tastes best, when served hot!

Slow Cooker Chinese Spare Ribs

- Prep time20 mins
- Cook time8 hours
- Total time8 hours 20 mins
- Serves: 4-6

Ingredients

- 4 lbs pork spare ribs
- 1 tablespoon Chinese five spice
- 1 tablespoon plus 1 teaspoon fresh grated ginger
- 2 teaspoons grated fresh grated garlic
- ¼ cup dry white wine or sherry
- 1 tablespoon plus 1 teaspoon apple cider vinegar
- 2 tablespoons coconut aminos or tamari (I used coconut aminos)
- 1 tablespoon tomato paste
- 1 tablespoon plus 1 teaspoon lemon juice
- optional 2 teaspoons of honey

How to make it

1. First take an oven grill or rack and put it in an oven, and place it a few inches from the direct source of heat.
2. Take a baking foil or sheet and keep a wire rack or grill and put the ribs on it.

3. Then take a small bowl or pot to mix Chinese spices, grated-ginger & garlic.
4. Also put sherry, white wine, apple cider vinegar, tamari, and paste of tomato, lemon juice and some honey.
5. Blend it well. After the broiler is hot enough, put the ribs and keep it under the broiler and cook it till it turns brown on each side.
6. Heat it for four to six minutes.
7. Now take the ribs in a crockpot and put the sauce on the sides of the ribs.
8. Heat the crockpot for around seven to eight hours after putting on the cover.
9. Keep the lid over the crockpot.
10. Enjoy, when it's done!

Easy Slow Cooker Kalua Pork

Ingredients

- 1 3-5 lb Pork Butt or Pork Shoulder
- 1 tbs liquid smoke
- 2-3 tbs red Hawaiian Sea Salt (use your discretion, using more if your roast is bigger)

How to make it

1. Begin with the pork and make some holes in the pork, the holes should be spread all over the pork.
2. Now put the pork butt in the crockpot and put liquid smoke over the pork.

3. Apply some Hawaiian sea salt over the pork.
4. Then set the crockpot to low and heat it for seven to twelve hrs.
5. The time depends upon the size of the pork.
6. After the pork is cooked, it would be very soft and could be shredded into smaller pieces by using a knife or a couple of forks.
7. You can serve it with rice or combine it with cabbage.
8. When using cabbage, do remember to use tamari for the aroma and flavor.
9. Also remember to keep some extra juices from the pork, to keep the pork dry.
10. This is only for the pork you plan to store for later use.

Slow Cooker Baby Back Ribs + Paleo BBQ Sauce

- Prep time: 45 mins
- Cook time: 6 hours
- Total time: 6 hours 45 mins

Ingredients

- 2 Cups Tomato Sauce
- ⅔ Cups Unsweetened Apple Sauce
- 4 Tablespoons Apple Cider Vinegar
- 4 Tablespoons Coconut Aminos

- 2 Tablespoons Dijon Mustard
- 2 teaspoons Hot Pepper Sauce (I like Trader Joe's Chili Pepper Sauce)
- ½ teaspoon black pepper
- 1 Tablespoon Ghee or GrassFed Butter
- 2 Cloves of Garlic, finely minced
- 2 teaspoons Chili Powder
- 1 teaspoon Paprika
- ½ teaspoon of cayenne (use more for extra SPICE!)
- 1 yellow onion, medium dice
- 2-3 lbs Pork Baby Back Ribs
- Salt, Pepper and Garlic Powder to taste

How to make it

1. First combine applesauce vinegar, tomato sauce, hot pepper sauce, and black pepper.
2. Then in a medium sized pot or saucepan put butter and heat it, so that the butter melts.
3. Keep the pot at medium heat, and put garlic, chili powder, paprika and cayenne, and combine it thoroughly to get the aroma.
4. Then blend in the tomato sauce and boil it.
5. Then remove the cover for half an hour, so that the moisture evaporates.
6. After that cool it down, and put it in glass jars or freezer jars fro refrigeration.
7. Other than that, put chopped yellow onion and put it at the base of the cooker.

8. Then generously apply pepper, salt, garlic powder on the ribs. Cut the racks into smaller pieces to put it into the crockpot and put a layer of BBQ sauce.
9. Then heat the crockpot for six to eight hours while setting the temperature to low, and see to it the meat should get separated from the bones.
10. Now your ribs are ready to be served with BBQ sauce.

Slow Cooker Balsamic Pulled Pork With Polenta

- Prep time10 mins
- Cook time6 hours
- Total time6 hours 10 mins
- Serves: 4-6

Ingredients

For the pork

- 2½ pound boneless pork loin
- ½ teaspoon kosher salt
- ¼ teaspoon ground pepper
- 3 cloves garlic, minced
- ½ teaspoon smoked paprika
- ½ teaspoon cumin
- ½ cup chicken broth
- ½ cup balsamic vinegar
- 2 tablespoons brown sugar
- 1 tablespoon soy sauce
- For the polenta

- 2 cups milk
- 2 cups water
- 1 teaspoon kosher salt
- 1 cup polenta (corn grits)
- 1 tablespoon butter
- ½ cup grated cheddar or monterey jack cheese
- For the avocado cream
- ½ avocado
- ½ cup plain Greek yogurt
- 2 tablespoons cilantro
- juice of ½ a lime
- salt& pepper

How to make it:-

1. First begin with the pork and mix all the spices like pepper, garlic, paprika cumin and some salt.
2. Apply it on the pork loin. Blend the rest of the items in a small mixing bowl or container and put it in the crockpot.
3. Then put the pork in the crockpot and heat for six hours while setting the temperature to low.
4. Take out the pork and make a few pieces with sharp utensils like a knife or forks.
5. And blend everything and put it again in the crockpot.
6. Now for making the polenta-Start by taking a saucepan or pot where the milk, salt and water have to be boiled.
7. After it's done, keep it aside for a few minutes and put the polenta in it. Heat it for ten minutes.

8. Then put the butter, season and cheese and put some salt in it.
9. And for the avocado cream- Take all the items in a food blender, and process it till it becomes soft.
10. At the end while serving it, put the polenta in the bottom of a serving bowl or serving pot and place the pork over it.
11. The cream should be applied over the pork, and cilantro, cheese can be used to decorate it.

Easy Slow Cooked

- Prep time: 5 mins
- Cook time: 8 hours
- Total time: 8 hours 5 mins
- Serves: 8

Ingredients :-

- 4-5 pound Boston Butt (also sold as "pork shoulder")
- 1/4 c Olive Oil
- 2 t Salt
- 1 t Pepper
- 1 T Dried Roseamry

How to make it :-

1. First take a crockpot and place the pork in it.
2. Then put the oil over it and apply it on the pork with your hands.
3. Add the spices over it and, and mix it well. Then clean your hands, and heat it for eight to ten hours while setting the heat to low.
4. Then make small pieces or shreds of the meat by using a couple of forks or knife. It is now ready to be served.

Slow Cooker Beef Rendang

Ingredients:

For the spice paste:

- 60g desiccated coconut, toasted in a dry wok
- 6 dried birds eye chillies
- 1 tsp ground cumin
- 2 tsp ground coriander
- 1 tsp turmeric powder
- 1 tsp salt
- 1/2 cup water
- 6 cloves garlic
- 4 shallots (small)
- 4 red chillies, deseeded

For the beef:

- 1 tbsp coconut oil
- 6 kafir lime leaves
- 2 stalks lemongrass, slit down the middle
- 160ml coconut cream
- 1 large cinnamon stick, broken in half
- 1 tbsp tamarind paste mixed in 120ml boiling water
- 15 drops stevia liquid
- 1 beef cheek cut into chunks
- 3 large pieces oxtail
- 1/2 cup cilantro leaves

How to make it :-

1. Take all the items and mix it in a blender, to make it gooey.
2. Then take a skillet where coconut oil has to be heated.
3. Then put the beef cheek & oxtail and fry it. Put the paste of spices and fry for more than one minute.
4. The put the remaining items other than cilantro and blend it properly.
5. Then put everything in a crock pot and heat it for around four to six hours while setting the temperature to high.
6. Then before it's served, put the cilantro leaves over it to embellish it.

7. It can also be served with cauliflower rice, rainbow chard and mashed swede.

Beef Bone Broth

Ingredients

- 4 qts filtered water
- 2lbs beef bones (ask butcher for soup bones)
- 1 Tbsp sea salt
- 3 garlic gloves, peeled and diced

How to make it

1. Set the temperature of the crock pot to high and put all the items in it.
2. Then boil the stock, and lower the heat.
3. Let the stock to be heated for half a day or more, could be kept for a full day also.
4. When it is finished, cool it off, and find a mesh or cheese cloth to drain the liquid.
5. Then keep the stock in the refrigerator. When it's cooled, skim the fat from the top of the broth. Do it properly and the final broth would be like a jelly.
6. Then keep the broth in glass jars for consuming it later.

Paleo Slow Cooker Breakfast Casserole

- 6 servings

Ingredients

- 2 tablespoons Coconut Oil
- 1 ⅓ cups slice Leek
- 2 teaspoons mince Garlic, Cloves
- 1 cup chop Kale
- 8 individual beat Egg
- ⅔ cups peel and grate Sweet Potato
- 1 ½ cups Homemade Beef Sausage –

Freezer Containers

- 1 Gallon Freezer Bag – Order Now!

How to make it

1. First take a skillet or frying pan and heat it to medium heat, and some coconut oil in it.
2. Put leeks, garlic, kale and fry.
3. Take a big pot or mixing bowl and add eggs, sweet potato, beef sausage and fried veggies.
4. Then take a crockpot and heat for around six hours while keeping the temperature set to low.
5. Then let it cool down and make it into pieces of the same size, and refrigerate it in freezer bags.
6. Put the name on the bag and refrigerate it to enjoy it later.

Crock Pot Beef Stew

Ingredients:-

- 2-3 lbsgrassfedbeed chuck roast, cut into 1 1/2" cubes
- salt& pepper
- 3 tbs coconut oil
- 3 medium onions chopped
- 1 6 ounce jar of tomato paste, I like to use Eden Organic because they have it in jars instead of cans
- 2 cups of homemade chicken or beef broth (I have made it with both)
- 3 tbs of coconut aminos
- 1 lb carrots, peeled and cut into 1" pieces (I used baby carrots in a bag)
- 1 lb parsnips, peeled and cut into 1" pieces
- 8 ounces of white mushrooms cut into 1" pieces
- 3 celery stocks cut into 1" pieces
- 2 tsp fresh thyme leaves
- 2 bay leaves
- 2 tbs of powered tapioca flour, (Is tapioca paleo? That is up to you to decided. Since I only use it to thicken stews I don't see why not.)

How to make it:

1. Take the beef and remove the moisture by paper towels.
2. Then apply pepper and salt over it.
3. Then use a skillet or pan where coconut oil has to be heated.

4. Then in the oil fry the beef till it changes color to brown.
5. Heat each side for three to four minutes.
6. Then put the things in crock pot and repeat the procedure.
7. Then put one tablespoon of oil, onions and some salt. Fry for another six to seven minutes.
8. Put some paste of tomato and heat for another couple of minutes.
9. Then put the broth and coconut aminos and soak for two or three minutes.
10. Take everything and place it over the beef in the slow cooker.
11. Blend in tapioca and bay leaves. Then put some carrots, parsnips, celery, mushroom, thyme and one tablespoon of coconut oil in it.
12. Then apply some pepper and salt over it.
13. Take a foil and put veggies in it, and place it over the meat.
14. After the veggie foil is kept, close the cover, and heat it for around six to seven hours while the temperature is set to high.
15. And ten to eleven hours if it's set to low.
16. When it's over, take the veggies out of the foil and place it over the beef directly, and blend it properly.
17. You can also put any other thing like potatoes in the foil instead of the vegetables.
18. Serve and relish!

Slow Cooker Spicy Indian Beef Roast

Ingredients

- 2 Red Onions, Chopped
- 2 Tbs coconut Oil
- 1 Tsp black Mustard Seeds
- 1 Tsp fine Sea Salt
- 2.5 Lbs grassfed Beef Roast (Chuck Blade)
- 25curry Leaves
- 2 Tbs Lemon Juice
- 2 Tbs Garlic, Minced Or Grated
- 1.5 Inch Ginger, Minced Or Grated
- 1 Serrano Pepper, Minced
- 1 Tbs meat Masala
- 1 Tbs coriander Powder
- 2 Tsp kashmiri Chili Powder
- 1 Tsp turmeric Powder
- ½ Tsp Freshly Groundblack Peppercorns
- ¼ Cup Coconut Slices Orcoconut Flakes

How to make it :-

1. Take a slow cooker and put onions, coconut oil, seeds of mustard and some salt.
2. Heat for around one hour and keep all other items ready.
3. Then put all other items other than the coconut flakes.

4. Then heat for another three hours.
5. Cut the meat into small pieces or shred it completely with a knife or fork.
6. Then heat it again for one more hour by setting the temperature to high.
7. The items can be added together or separately as mentioned above, mixing it later will let the flavor blend in more.
8. Serve and relish!

Picadillo Paleo

Ingredients:

- 2 pounds ground beef (grass-fed is best)
- 1 pound cooked nitrite-free chicken sausages, diced
- 1 1/2 tablespoons chilli powder
- 2 teaspoons ground cumin
- 1 tablespoon dried oregano
- 1 teaspoon cinnamon
- 2 14.5 oz cans diced tomatoes, drained slightly
- 1 6 oz can tomato paste
- 1 1/2 red onions, diced
- 2 chopped and seeded Anaheim peppers (leave some seeds in if you want more of a kick)
- 1 chopped and seeded poblano pepper
- 20 green olives, chopped
- 8 cloves of garlic, minced
- Salt and pepper, to taste

- How to make it:

How to make it :-

1. Take a skillet and put beef in it, and heat it till it becomes brown.
2. Take out the beef liquid and put it in the crock pot. Put all items except the salt.
3. Blend and heat for six to eight hours by setting the temperature to low.
4. Later on salt can put after all other aromas have blended in, then you can serve it with chopped tomatoes, chicken sausages, and your Picadillo is ready to served!

Meaty Paleo Chili

Ingredients

- 600 grams of ground beef
- 600 grams of stew meat (chunks of beef)
- 2 onions, chopped
- 2 green pepperoncini, chopped
- 1 red and 1 green bell pepper, chopped
- 6 cloves of garlic, finely chopped
- 1 can of tomatoes (8oz/ 240gm)
- 2-3 Tablespoons chili powder
- 3 Thai chilies finely chopped or 1 Tablespoon dried chili flakes

- 1 cup bone broth (or water)
- salt to taste

How to make it :-

1. First in a skillet fry onions, pepperoncini, bell peppers, garlic in coconut oil.
2. Then put in the crockpot later on.
3. On the skillet heat the ground beef till it changes color to brown, and put it in the crock pot, repeat the same procedure with the beef chunks.
4. At the end put everything in the crock pot and heat for three to four hours.
5. And it takes around one to two hours in a stove pot. It tastes better when it's heated for a longer duration.
6. Apply chili, avocado, diced tomatoes, cilantro, diced onions, green onion, grated cheese, and sour cream.
7. Yogurt can also be put instead of cheese; you could also put sweet potatoes to make it taste better.

Slow Cooker Pot Roast

Serves: 6

Ingredients :-

- 2 pound beef arm or chuck roast, trimmed of excess fat
- 1 1/2 teaspoons kosher sea salt
- 3/4 teaspoon freshly ground black pepper
- 2 tablespoons finely chopped fresh basil
- 1/2 cup finely chopped yellow onion
- 4 cloves garlic, finely minced
- 2 bay leaves
- 2 cups beef stock, preferably homemade

How to make it :-

1. Take beef roast to start with and remove the moisture with a paper towel and apply pepper, salt, basil on all sides.
2. Put the roast on a slow cooker and apply the onions and garlic on it.
3. Then put the beef stock, from the sides and also place some bay leaves.
4. Then heat it for eight to ten hours while setting the temperature to low.
5. The meat should become soft and the bay leaves can be taken out if not needed, and can be put later.

Paleo Slow Cooker Shin Beef

Ingredients

- 440g grass-fed shin beef
- Grassfed beef dripping
- 2 Carrots
- 1 Onion
- 3 Celery sticks
- 200ml Beef stock
- Cumin
- Salt and pepper
- 1/2 celeriac
- Mixed winter herbs (thyme/ bay leaf/ parsley)

How to make it:-

1. Take the beef and heat it in a skillet or pan to make it brown.
2. Then take it out of the pan and do the same thing with the veggies.
3. Now in a crockpot put all the items, and also put stock and spices.
4. Set the temperature to low and heat it for around eight hours.
5. Mince and peel the celeriac and use apply it on the beef and cook it for twenty mins.
6. After it's finished, take the small meat pieces in the crockpot and in the skillet the juices should be lessened to make it slightly thick or gravy like.
7. Before serving, take out the celeriac and give a bowl of gravy and shin beef.
8. Now it's ready to be savored!

Slow Cooker Pork Stew W Oyster Mushrooms

Ingredients

- 2 tbsplard or coconut oil
- 1 medium onion, chopped
- 1 clove garlic, chopped
- 2lbs pork loin, cut into 1" cubes and patted dry
- 1/2 tsp Himalayan salt
- 1/2 tsp freshly cracked black pepper
- 2 tbsp dried oregano
- 2 tbsp dried mustard
- 1/2 tsp freshly ground whole nutmeg
- 1 1/2 cups bone broth
- 2 tbsp white wine vinegar
- 2 lbs oyster mushrooms
- 1/4 cup full fat coconut milk
- 1/4 cup ghee
- 3 tbsp capers

How To Make It

1. Heat a skillet or a frying pan. Put the meat side by side and they shouldn't touch each other.
2. Heat it till the point the color changes to brown.
3. Do not put all the pieces at once, and then take the cooked meat in a pot or bowl.
4. The juices would come out of the meat and settle at the bottom of the pot.

5. After it has finished keep it side and lower the heat of the skillet to medium, and put some fat in it.
6. Then fry the garlic and onions in the fat, till the point the onion is transformed into translucent bits and the aroma is evident.
7. Put oregano, mustard, nutmeg and blend it, put some white wine and broth in it.
8. Then put the meat and juices in the pan, and let it soak and take it out and put it in the slow cooker.
9. And set the temperature of the crock pot to low and heat it for six hours if the temperature is set to low and four hours if it's set to high.
10. Put mushrooms in it, and some more water, and keep on heating it for another hour if the temperature is set to high or two hours if it is set to low.
11. Then use a dipper or ladle some of the liquid in another pot or bowl, then blend in coconut milk, ghee and again put it in the crock pot.
12. Put a few capers in it. And it's ready to be enjoyed!

Slow Cooker Chicken Yellow Curry Soup

Ingredients

- 1-1/2 lb. (~700 g) boneless chicken breasts or thighs, cut into chunks
- 6 cups of veggies, chopped (I used one cup each of onion, carrots, green beans, broccoli, tomatoes and

red bell pepper. Use what you like or have on hand.)
- 1-14 oz can (~400 ml) of full fat coconut milk
- 1 cup crushed tomatoes (or tomato sauce)
- 1 Tablespoon cumin
- 2 teaspoons ground coriander
- 2 teaspoons ground ginger
- 2 teaspoons garlic powder
- 1 teaspoon cinnamon
- ½ teaspoon cayenne pepper, optional
- 1 cup water (for a thicker, curry-like sauce, omit the water)
- Salt, to taste

How to make it

1. Take the crockpot and use a sharp knife to cut the chicken and vegetables into pieces.
2. Place it in the slow cooker.
3. And blend in coconut milk, tomatoes which are crushed.
4. Put some spices like ginger, garlic, cumin, coriander, cinnamon and cayenne pepper.
5. Put some water in it and blend everything.
6. Heat for around five to six hours. To have semi-liquid gravy and not too much liquid, then put less water, around one cup.
7. Uncover the lid to let the moisture to get out for the last one hour of cooking.
8. Put some salt according to taste. It would taste nice with cauliflower rice or by itself.

9. You can now enjoy your curry soup.

Crockpot Stuffed Chicken Breasts

4 – 6 servings

Ingredients:

- 4 – 6 boneless chicken breasts
- 1 T olive oil or fat of choice
- ½ onion, diced
- ½ red pepper, cut into thin strips
- 2 pepperoncini peppers, cut into thin strips
- 6 oz fresh spinach
- 2 tsp minced garlic
- 1 ½ tsp fresh oregano or ½ tsp dried oregano
- salt and pepper
- squeeze of lemon
- 1 cup chicken stock
- ½ cup white wine (optional, but highly recommended. It imparts amazing flavor throughout the chicken)
- 1/3 cup feta cheese, if you tolerate dairy. If not, leave out.
- Optional Toppings: fresh parsley, fresh oregano, or fresh mint, squeeze of fresh lemon

How to make it:

1. First take the chicken breast and use a knife to cut through the chicken, make a thin cut, so that a pocket can be made.
2. Put pepper and salt on both sides of the chicken.
3. Then take a skillet or a frying pan where you have to fry olive oil at moderate heat.
4. Then put onions and pepper for a couple of minutes.
5. Then put spinach and garlic in it, heat it till the point that the spinach gets wilted.
6. Put dry oregano and hint of pepper and salt, and take it out from the heat.
7. Feta can be put inside the chicken if needed; it should be put totally inside the chicken.
8. And put some pepper or spinach inside the chicken breasts.
9. Take a crockpot and put the stuffed chicken in the crockpot and add some lemon juice on the chicken.
10. Put some juice of lemon on the chicken.
11. Also put the stock of chicken and wine in the crockpot.
12. Put the cover over it and set the temperature to low for six to eight hours, and high fir around four hours.
13. Add some garnishing to make it better!

Lemon & Artichoke Slow Cooker Chicken

- Yield: Serves 6 - 8

- NF based on 1 of 8 servings

Ingredients

The Spice Blend

- 1 teaspoonras el hanout
- (orgaram masala)
- 1/2 teaspoon turmeric
- 1/2 teaspoon red pepper flakes
- 1/2 teaspoon ground cumin
- 1/2 teaspoon ground ginger
- 1/4 teaspoon ground cinnamon
- 1/4 teaspoon freshly cracked black pepper
- 1/4 teaspoon Himalayan salt

The Chicken

- 2 whole chickens (approx. 4lb each), cut into 10 pieces each (breasts cut in half, thighs, legs and wings)
- Salt and pepper to taste
- 2 tablespoons ghee
- 1 large onion, diced
- 4 cloves garlic, chopped
- 2 cups light chicken stock
- 1/4 cup fresh lemon juice
- the zest of 2 lemons

The Add-ons

- 2 lemons, sliced
- 2 cans artichoke hearts, rinsed, drained and cut in half

- 1 cup caper berries, rinsed
- 2 tablespoons tapioca flour + 2 tablespoons water
- 2 tablespoons fresh parsley, chopped

How To Make It

1. Prepare the chicken in a liquid of eight cups of water, quarter cup of salt, and then squeeze two pieces of lemons and shells of two lemons.
2. Then take all the items in a small mixing bowl or container, and mix the spices and blend the mixture.
3. Then take the chicken and cut it into pieces, cut everything into two pieces each.
4. And drizzle some pepper and salt. Take a big frying pan and give some heat and let the ghee melt.
5. Then put the pieces of chicken, few pieces at once, fry till the color changes to golden brown and it becomes crumbly.
6. And cook each side for four to five minutes.
7. Then transfer the chicken to the slow cooker.
8. Then fry the onions and garlic at moderate temperature, the onions become translucent.
9. Put some chicken stock, lemon juice, lemon zest and blend of spices.
10. Then pour it over the chicken.
11. Then switch on the slow cooker and heat for five to seven hours.

12. Put the lemon slices and artichoke hearts and berries, an hour before it would be taken out.
13. After it finishes, take out all the items and put it in a big bowl or pot, and heat it at low, to keep it warm.
14. Remove the excess liquid through a strainer into a saucepan.
15. Put the tapioca in two tablespoons of water and put it over the soaked in stock.
16. Then boil it at high temperature for around one or two minutes, blending constantly, till the point the sauce becomes thick.
17. At the end before serving, put the sauce on the chicken and enjoy.

Easy Crock Pot Roasted Chicken w/ Lemon Parsley Butter

- Yield: Approximately 6 - 8 servings

Ingredients

- 1 Whole Roasting Chicken (5 - 6lbs depending on your crock pot size)
- 1 cup water
- 1/2 tsp kosher salt
- 1/4 tso ground black pepper
- 1 whole lemon, sliced thinly

- 4 Tbl butter or ghee
- 2 Tbl chopped fresh parsley

How to make it

1. First clean the chicken with water, and take out anything else inside the chicken.
2. Take pepper and salt and apply it over the chicken.
3. Then in the slow cooker put the chicken and in it and add water.
4. The water should only cover the base and put more water if the crockpot is big.
5. Heat it for three hours and set the temperature to high. The temperature inside the slow cooker and near to the chicken's thigh should be around 165 Degrees Fahrenheit.
6. To check whether the chicken is done, the chicken shouldn't be pink and juices should be clean.
7. Put butter, parsley and pieces of lemon in the slow cooker for around ten minutes.
8. You could heat it separately in another pan with lemon and butter, till the time lemon becomes dark and the butter melts.
9. And add it over the chicken before eating or serving.

Crock-Pot Kalua Chicken Tacos With Chili Lime Mango Salsa

•Yield: Serves 4

Ingredients

Kalua Chicken:

- 1.5-2lbs of boneless skinless chicken thighs
- 1 tbs Hawaiian sea salt
- 1 tbs liquid smoke

Chili Lime Mango Salsa:

- 1 large mango, chopped
- 2 stalks of green onion, chopped
- 6 sprigs of cilantro, diced
- Juice of 1 lime
- 1 tsp chili powder

Other ingredients:

- Guacamole (fresh or store bought)
- Corn tortillas
- If you're grain-free you can sub in butter lettuce leaves or a leaf of your choice for the tortillas!

How to make it

1. At first begin with a crockpot and set the temperature to low.

2. Then put the chicken thighs, and Hawaiian sea salt.
3. Also you should put some liquid smoke.
4. The coating over the chicken thighs should be perfect and heat it for five hours, while keeping the temperature set to low.
5. Take two sharp utensils or forks to for shredding the chicken. Simultaneously, make your salsa dip in a mixing bowl, by putting mango, onions, cilantro, lime and chili.
6. Keep it aside for quarter of an hour.
7. And when the both preparations are ready, put both the chicken and salsa in the tortillas.
8. You chicken tacos are ready to be enjoyed!

Slow Cooked Gizzard Recipe

Ingredients

- 1 bunch of organic cilantro, washed and cleaned from stems
- 3 large cloves of organic garlic, peeled and sliced
- 1 small organic onion
- 1 pound of free range chicken gizzards
- ¼ cup Passata di Pomodoro
- ½ cup white wine
- ¼ cup water
- a good pinch of celtic sea salt

How to make it

1. Take a crockpot and put all the items in it and blend it properly.
2. The gizzards should be moistened and partially dipped in the liquid.
3. While serving, use cassava flour or cauliflower rice. Before that it has to be heated for six hours, with the temperature set to low.

Slow Cooker Lemon Chicken Thighs

- Prep time: 10 minutes
- Cook time: 7 hours on low

Ingredients

- 2 large carrots, peeled and chopped
- 1/2 cup chopped yellow onion
- 2 pounds bone-in, skin-on chicken thighs
- 4 cloves garlic, minced
- 1/4 teaspoon salt
- black pepper to taste
- 1/2 tablespoon ground sage
- 1/2 tablespoon rosemary
- juice of one lemon
- 1 tablespoon extra virgin olive oil

How to make it

1. Take a crockpot of around two gallons.
2. Put carrots & onions in it.

3. Put the chicken over the vegetables and the skin should be pointing upwards.
4. Then put garlic, herbs and seasonings.
5. Take out the lemon juice into the crock pot, sprinkle some virgin olive oil in it.
6. Then set the temperature to low and heat it for around 7 hours.
7. When the chicken becomes soft and gets separated from the bone, take it out.
8. And it is ready to be served!

Slow Cooker Basic Chicken Stock

- Prep:5mins
- Cook:24 hours
- Total:24 hours 5 mins
- Serves: 14

Ingredients

- 2 or more (see NOTES) chicken carcasses from roasted chicken plus any raw backs, necks and wings
- 1 Tablespoon apple cider vinegar
- 20 cups filtered water
- 2 Tablespoon kosher salt
- 6 to 6.5 Quart slow cooker
- fine mesh strainer
- mason jars or other glass storage containers

How to make it

1. Take a crockpot and put chicken parts in it. Put some water and apple cider vinegar.
2. Keep it aside for around half an hour or 45mins.
3. Set the cooker to high and put some kosher salt in it. It should be heated for around four hours.
4. When it's done, open the cover and skim the top.
5. And again set the temperature to low for around eighteen to twenty hours.
6. Do not stop the heat in between.
7. After the stock is finished, and has been cooled down, use a mesh to strain it in a big sup bowl.
8. Use some tong or spoon to remove any bones or parts.
9. You can refrigerate it by keeping it in freezer jars, but do not keep it in refrigerator, till the time it cools off completely.

Crockpot Chicken Cacciatore

- Prep:· 10 mins
- Cook:· 4 hours
- Total:· 4 hours 10 mins
- Serves: 6

Ingredients

- 2 pounds assorted skinless chicken parts (I used 6 bone-in, skinless chicken legs and 5 boneless, skinless chicken thighs)
- 2 teaspoons kosher salt
- ½ teaspoon fresh ground black pepper
- 1 sprig fresh rosemary
- ¼ cup whole wheat flour
- ¼ cup white wine
- 1 celery rib, thinly sliced
- 2 small or 1 medium yellow onion, thinly sliced into half moons
- 8 ounces crimini mushrooms, stems removed, quartered
- 1 28-ounce can whole plum tomatoes in juice (unsalted)

How to make it

1. Do the preparation by defrosting the chicken, and put it in the crockpot.
2. Drizzle pepper and salt.
3. Cleanse the mushrooms with water and chop each into four pieces.
4. Again cleanse the celery and chop off the base and the top.
5. Cut it into moon shaped pieces.
6. Take the skin of the onion out and cut it into two pieces.
7. Then make half moon pieces from it.

8. Then in another container take wine and flour.
9. Take some rosemary and pour a can of tomatoes.
10. For cooking take the crock pot first, and put the flour on the chicken and the wine in it.
11. Then put pieces of celery, the mushrooms, onions, then finally the can of tomatoes.
12. Do not blend or mix. Set the temperature of the crockpot to high and heat it for four hours.
13. And when it's finished the aroma from the freshly cooked cacciatore will enthrall you.

Crock Pot Chicken Stock

- Serves: about 2 quarts

Ingredients

- 1 organic chicken carcass
- 1 medium onion, quartered
- 3 carrots, quartered
- 3 celery stalks, quartered
- 1 tablespoon apple cider vinegar
- filtered water to cover

How to make it

1. Take everything in the crockpot and set the temperature to low.
2. Heat the crockpot for twelve to eighteen hours.
3. Then strain the stock and keep it for refrigeration.

Paleo Chicken Tortilla Soup Recipe

- •Serves: 6

Ingredients

- 2 large chicken breasts, skin removed and cut into ½ inch strips
- 1 28oz can of diced tomatoes
- 32 ounces organic chicken broth
- 1 sweet onion, diced
- 2 jalepenos, de-seeded and diced
- 2 cups of shredded carrots
- 2 cups chopped celery
- 1 bunch of cilantro chopped fine
- 4 cloves of garlic, minced - I always use one of these
- 2 Tbs tomato paste
- 1 tsp chili powder
- 1 tsp cumin
- sea salt & fresh cracked pepper to taste
- olive oil
- 1-2 cups water

How to make it

1. At first take a slow cooker and heat it at moderate-high heat, keep some olive oil and quarter cup chicken broth.
2. Then put some garlic, onions, jalapeno, pepper and sea salt.
3. Heat everything till everything becomes tender.

4. Put rest of the items and water till the edge of the slow cooker.
5. Then put the lid on and heat for two hours or so at low heat.
6. Add salt and pepper as per taste.
7. When the chicken is fully cooked, shred it completely.
8. Use sharp knife or fork to do it.
9. Use pieces of avocado and cilantro for seasoning.
10. No need to put cheese or tortilla chips for taste, as it can be relished by itself.

Slow Cooker Paleo Chicken Soup Recipe

- Serves: 4

Ingredients

- 3 lbs of chicken parts, local free range when possible
- 3 quarts of water
- 4 stalks of celery
- 2 carrots
- 1½ tsp of minced garlic (you can use more if you are stuffed up)
- handful or fresh baby spinach
- 1 cup of pearl onions (I used frozen)
- thyme, rosemary, salt, pepper to taste

How to make it

1. At first skin the chicken.
2. Then add water in the crockpot.
3. Also put all the items in it other than rosemary and thyme.
4. Heat it for eight to ten hours.
5. Then take out the carrots, chicken, onions and celery. Separate the bones from the chicken.
6. And then put everything in a crockpot and then put the thyme and rosemary.
7. Set the heat to high and heat it for around half an hour.
8. Put the spinach till it droops because of the heat.
9. Your chicken soup is ready to be savored!

Crockpot Chicken Stock

- Prep time   5 mins
- Cook time   8 hours
- Total time   8 hours 5 mins

Ingredients

- 1 Chicken Carcass (A Bit Of Meat On The Bones Is Fine)
- 1 Onion
- 3-4 Bay Leaves
- 2-3 Tbsp Salt
- Ground Pepper (Optional)
- Water

How to make it

1. Take a crockpot and put the carcass in it. If you want put some bay leaves, salt, pepper and some onions in it.
2. Fill it with water till the edge of the pot leaving around an inch of space and heat it for eight to ten hours by putting the lid over it.
3. Then by using a slotted spoon separate the vegetables and bones.
4. You could also put some meat from the chicken, and finally you can refrigerate it, by giving some space or room to let it expand without damaging the glass jar.

Homemade Chicken Variation)

Ingredients:

- Bones from one free-range, organic chicken, include the wings and neck if possible
- Up to one pound of chicken feet
- 4 quarts of cold filtered water (Use more or less as needed to cover the ingredients.)
- 2 Tablespoons apple cider vinegar
- 1 large onion, cut into quarters
- 2-3 carrots, peeled and cut into 2 inch pieces
- 2-3 celery sticks, cut into 2 inch pieces
- 4-5 cloves of garlic, smashed
- 12 peppercorns

- 2 dried bay leave
- Feel free to add any other vegetable scraps you may have.

How to make it

1. Take all the items in a big crock pot and keep it in the cooker for half an hour or nearly an hour.
2. Put a lid over and heat for half a day by setting the heat to low.
3. The broth or stock has to be checked and water has to put into the stock if it gets dry.
4. After the stock is done, take the stock on a sieve. Then for a few hours it has to refrigerate.
5. Take out or separate any fat that comes to the top.
6. After this procedure is done, it can be refrigerated for around four to five days or more.

Slow Cooker Mexican Chicken Soup

Ingredients

- 6 cups Homemade Chicken Stock (or Broth) – View Recipe
- 1 ½ cups dice Carrot
- ⅔ cups dice Onion, Red
- 4 teaspoons mince Garlic, Cloves
- ½ cups dice Roma Tomato
- ¼ cups seed and dice Jalapeño
- 1 ¾ cups Tomato Juice
- 1 tablespoon Cumin

- 1 teaspoon Coriander, Ground
- 1 tablespoon Chili Powder
- 2 teaspoons Sea Salt
- ½ cups chop Cilantro, Fresh
- 4 cups cook and dice Chicken, Boneless Breasts
- 2 tablespoons juice Lime
- 1 cup peel, pit, and slice Avocado *(serving day)*

Freezer Containers

- 2 Gallon Freezer Bags –

How to make it

1. First take all the items other than avocado in crockpot.
2. Now heat it for six to eight hours.
3. Then put sliced avocado on top after it has been cooked.
4. Separate all the prepared items to refrigerate in freezer bags, but keep the avocado aside while refrigerating it.
5. On the day when it would be served put the frozen items in the crockpot and heat for six to eight hours, and put pieces of avocado over it.

Slow Cooker Chocolate Chicken Mole

- Prep time15 mins
- Cook time6 hours

- Total time6 hours 15 mins
- Serves: 6

Ingredients

- 2 lbs chicken pieces (breasts and legs work well) bone in, Skin removed
- salt and pepper
- 2 tbspghee
- 1 medium onion, chopped
- 4 cloves garlic, crushed or minced
- 6 - 7 whole tomatoes, peeled, seeded and chopped
- 5 dried New Mexico chili peppers, rehydrated and chopped
- ¼ cup almond butter
- 2.5 ozdark chocolate (70% or above)
- 1 teaspoon sea salt
- 1 teaspoon cumin powder
- ½ teaspoon cinnamon powder
- ½ tspguajillpo chili powder
- avocado, cilantro and jalapeno, all chopped.

How to make it

1. First put some ghee in a skillet or pan, it temperature should moderate.
2. Put some salt and pepper over the chicken.
3. After the ghee is slightly hot, place the chicken and fry it till the point the color changes to brown from each side.
4. You could do it slowly by taking small portions.
5. No take a crockpot and put the chicken in it.

6. Put some onions in the skillet and fry it for less than two minutes.
7. Then repeat the same process with garlic.
8. Then take the items and put it in the crock pot.
9. Then put some chili peppers, dark chocolate, almond butter, tomatoes, pepper and some salt in it.
10. Then heat the crockpot for four to six hours, till the time the chicken becomes soft and gets separated.
11. Then put some seasoning of avocado, cilantro and jalapeno to make it better.
12. Now it's ready to be relished.

Slow Cooker Coconut Curried Chicken

Ingredients

- 3 pounds of chicken (breasts, thighs, chicken on the bone, etc)
- 1 large onion chopped
- 2 carrots chopped small
- 2 clove garlic minced
- 1 Tbsp curry powder
- 1 Tbsp mustard (condiment, not the spice)
- 1/2 cup coconut cream (liquid) or milk
- 1/2 cup chicken stock
- 2 Tbsp ghee or butter
- salt to taste

How to make it

1. Take a slow cooker to begin with then in it put carrot, garlic and onion.
2. The chicken pieces can be put over the veggies and the chicken can be put in layers over it.
3. Put the spices on the chicken.
4. And take a small container where melted ghee can be blended with coconut cream and chicken stock.
5. Then it could be put on the chicken and you could heat it for six hours while keeping the temperature set to low.
6. After the chicken is finished, to make the gravy the chicken pieces can be taken out and you can take a hand blender and combine the puree.
7. You can put in a refrigerator and enjoy it after some time.

Balsamic Pot Roast Gravy with Roasted Garlic Mash.

Ingredients:

- Balsamic Pot Roast:
- 1 beef pot roast, about 2.5 pounds, tied with twine
- Sea salt + cracked black pepper
- 1 vidalia or sweet onion, chopped
- 2 tablespoons chopped fresh rosemary

- 2 tablespoons chopped fresh thyme
- 1/3 cup chopped roasted garlic (about 2-3 heads' worth)
- 1 cup red wine (or beef broth, for Whole30)
- 1/2 cup balsamic vinegar
- 1 tablespoon ghee
- Roasted Garlic Mash:
- 1 head cauliflower, cut into florets
- 1 pound parsnips, peeled and cut into 1 inch segments
- 1/4 cup roasted garlic (about 1-2 heads' worth)
- 3 tablespoons ghee
- 1/2 teaspoon sea salt
- 1/4 teaspoon pepper

How to make it:

1. Begin with a big crock pot and put the beef pot roast in it. Then drizzle some pepper and salt over it.
2. Take one mixing container or bowl where the onion rosemary, thyme, red wine or beef broth, balsamic vinegar or roasted garlic are blended together.
3. Then take the preparation and heat it for around six hours, changing the sides of the roast from one side to another.
4. After the cooking the meat, take it out of the crockpot and mince it with sharp utensil.
5. Some ghee could be put in the sauce it could be near about a tablespoon.

6. After that use a food blender to blend the mix and make it soft.
7. And take the minced roast and mix it with the sauce and heat it for a few minutes, put some salt and pepper if needed.
8. Then in another container or mixing bowl boil salted water and put cauliflower and parsnips. It should be cooked for ten minutes or till the point that everything in it becomes soft.
9. Then drain out the excess liquid.
10. Put the ghee, salt, pepper or roasted garlic in the veggies.
11. Ghee can be added as per need or taste then take the food blender and blend till gets soft or smooth.
12. At the end, over the mash of roasted garlic you can pour the pot roast gravy.

Easy Paleo Pot

Ingredients

- Approximately 2.5 lb chuck roast
- salt and pepper to taste
- 2 cloves of garlic, roughly chopped
- 1/2 cup onion, roughly chopped
- 2 cups chopped celery
- 1 cup baby carrots (or chopped carrots)
- 2 cups of water or broth
- (optional) 1 cup red wine

- 2 Tbl fresh parsley, chopped

How to make it

1. Take the roast in a heated up pan and before that sprinkle some pepper and salt.
2. Fry it till the color changes to brown.
3. Then put it in a slow cooker with a lid and put each and every item in it other than the parsley.
4. Close the lid and heat it for five hours or so.
5. Check the flavor and seasoning with pepper and salt.
6. Then put some parsley on top of rutabaga and cauliflower puree to decorate it.
7. After this is done, it's ready to be savored.

Crockpot Pork Roast

- Prep time·   5 mins
- Cook time   4 hours
- Total time   4 hours 5 mins

Ingredients

- 3-4 lb pork butt roast
- ¼ cup coconut aminos

- favorite spice blend (I used a homemade one that had onion powder, garlic powder, black pepper, and salt in it)

How to make it

1. Begin with a crockpot and put the pork roast in it.
2. Then add coconut aminos, and drizzle a lot of spices, and blend well.
3. Then it has be heated for four to six hours with the temperature set to low, and cut the roast into pieces, or it has to be shredded.
4. After that the preparation is ready to be relished.

Pot Roast Soup

- Prep Time   15 min
- Cook Time   8 hr
- Total Time   8 hr 15 min

Ingredients

- 1.25 lb Stew Meat
- 1 Large Onion, Big Dice
- 3 Carrots, Big Dice
- 1/2 Medium Butter nut squash, Big Dice

- 1 14oz Can of Diced Tomatoes
- a little less than 8oz of Mushrooms, Big Dice
- ~3/4 Cup Chicken Stock
- Dried Basil, Oregano, Cumin
- Splash of Apple Cider Vinegar
- Salt + Pepper

How to make it

1. Take all the veggies in the beginning, and put them one by one from the base of a slow cooker.
2. Put the stew meat and cut it up in pieces if the pieces are quite big.
3. The spices are to be blended in, like salt and pepper, chicken stock with a can of tomatoes; the tomato juice is also essential.
4. Pour some apple cider vinegar also.
5. Blend it well, and heat it for eight hours if the temperature is set to low and five hours if it's set to high.

Kendra's Paleo Pot Roast

Ingredients:

- 3-4 lb bottom round roast (mine was 4lbs)
- 4-5 cloves garlic, mashed and diced (or minced)

- seasonings: I had some fresh thyme and some dried oregano I sprinkled on, use what you have or what sounds good
- olive oil or grapeseed oil, enough to cover the bottom of the pan (~1-2 Tbsp)
- 1 large onion, diced
- 2-3 celery stalks, chopped into bite size pieces
- 2-3 medium carrots, peeled and sliced into bite size pieces
- 2-3 parsnips, peeled and chopped into bite size pieces
- 1 cup dry red wine
- 1/2 cup beef broth or chicken stock (I used chicken b/c I had some to use up).
- salt& pepper to taste

How to make it:

1. Begin with setting the oven temperature to 325 Degrees Fahrenheit.
2. Then on the roast apply garlic paste and add some salt and pepper.
3. You could drizzle some oregano.
4. Now take a cooking pot and put oil in it, and the temperature set to medium.
5. And now cover the pot, take the roast in the oil and cook it till it gets brown from each side, around a couple of minutes per side.
6. The edges have to be fried till the point the meat locks in the moisture.

7. After the meat has changed color we have to put the veggies and the thyme.
8. Before heating it in the oven you have to add the wine and the liquid broth over the meat and cover the pot.
9. At the set temperature heat it for around two to three hours.
10. While using a crockpot remember to set the temperature to low, and have to keep it in the oven for the day.
11. The snail paced cooking style separates the meat, and the aroma is splendid as it helps to settle down all the ingredients perfectly.
12. Now your pot roast is ready to be relished upon.

Ham & Sweet Potato Slow Cooker Quittata

Serves: 8

Ingredients

- 12 eggs
- 2 c. sweet potato, steamed and diced (or raw and shredded)
- 1 c. coconut milk, full fat (gives the frittata more of a custardy texture)
- ½ lb ham (or any meat)
- ½ c. red onion, chopped
- ½ tsp sea salt

- ¼ tsp black pepper (optional)

How to make it

1. First start with taking a big pot or bowl where coconut milk, eggs , salt and pepper are combined together.
2. They have to be blended perfectly.
3. Take a crock pot and put the above blended mix in the crock pot.
4. Then put potato, onions and ham across the mix.
5. Close the lid and heat it for two and half hours, the temperature should be set to high.
6. To prepare it faster you could take out the coconut milk and heat it for around one and half around.
7. When the stipulated time is over, your quittata is ready to be served!

Onion & Bison Soup

Ingredients:

- 6 large red onions, julienned 1/4" thick
- 2 lb. bison roast
- 2 quarts beef stock (highly recommend homemade here)
- 1/2 cup sherry
- 3 or more sprigs thyme
- 1 bay leaf

- 2 tbsp olive oil, plus additional to garnish
- salt and pepper to taste

How to make it:

1. First you should take a crock pot and put roast of bison and stock of beef, bay leaf and thyme.
2. Heat it keeping the temperature set to high and heat for around six hours otherwise set the temperature to low and leave it for the night.
3. Take the bison roast out and make shreds or small pieces from the roast.
4. Then put some onions and pour olive oil in a big pot where it's heated between medium-high heat.
5. Keep on blending it, and heat it till the volume of the onions become very less.
6. Then put some sherry and let the heat get reduced to medium and heat it for three minutes.
7. Then mix the beef stock and lower the heat and let it get mixed for three quarters of an hour.
8. Put some pepper or salt on the top and sprinkle some olive oil before serving it.
9. And your onion and bison soup is ready to be savored!

Rabbit & Andouille Sausage Stew

Ingredients:

- 1 rabbit
- 1 lb. andouille sausage, or other spicy smoked sausage, cut into 1/2 inch chunks
- 1 large onion, diced
- 6 medium carrots, unpeeled and cut into 1 inch chunks
- 8 oz. mushrooms
- 2 qt. chicken stock
- 1/4 tsp. red pepper flakes
- 1/4 tsp. cayenne
- 1/2 tsp. fresh ground black pepper
- 1/4 tsp. paprika
- 1 tbsp. coconut oil or ghee

How to make it:

1. The limbs of the rabbit have to be removed, and take a large skillet or pan where it has to be heated or fried in oil till the color changes to brown from each and every side.
2. And the heat should be set at medium or high setting.
3. Take the rabbit out if the pan and put onion, spices, sausage into the pan.
4. Then put quarter cup of chicken stock in the pan or skillet to deglaze it.
5. Then heat it for two minutes and saute onions till they become transparent.
6. Blend it in a crock pot with the temperature set to high and put the rabbit and rest of the items in it and cook it for six hours or so.

Coconut Lamb Curry

Ingredients

- 1 tablespoon coconut oil
- 700 grams diced lamb (a little fat on the meat is fine)
- 1 large brown onion
- ½ long red chilli
- 2 medium celery sticks, diced
- 3 cloves garlic, diced
- 2½ teaspoons garam masala powder
- 1¼ teaspoons turmeric powder
- 1 teaspoon fennel seeds
- 1½ teaspoons ghee (or extra coconut if avoiding dairy)
- 400ml coconut milk (1 can)
- 1½ tablespoons tomato paste
- 1 cup water
- 1⅓ teaspoon sea salt
- 2 medium carrots, diced
- Squeeze of lime or lemon juice
- Fresh coriander (cilantro) or parsley to garnish

How to make it

1. Take a big pot or saucepan and put a tablespoon of coconut oil and heat it.
2. Take some lamb and blend till the color changes to brown, like for three or four minutes, then we have to put the onion, celery and chili and heat it for around a minute, till it gets soft.
3. Then the heat should be brought down to medium.
4. Put some garam masala, turmeric, and seeds of fennel, ghee and garlic and blend it properly. Heat it for another minute.
5. Then put some coconut milk, seas salt, and water and tomato paste.You have to boil and blend it.
6. Change the heat setting to low so that the water is soaked, and heat it for an hour, use a spoon to blend it a few times, and while heating keep it covered.
7. After that put small chopped up chunks of carrots and heat it again for another half an hour or more. Blend it again a few times.
8. When it has been cooked fully, spray some coriander or parsley and pour some lime or lemon juice.
9. You can always eat and serve it with rice, vegetables or cauliflower as per your wish.

Slow Cooker Honey-Vanilla Applesauce

- Prep time: 30 mins
- Cook time: 5 hours

- Total time: 5 hours 30 mins
- Serves: 16

Ingredients

- About five pounds of apples, cored and quartered (and peeled if the skins are tough)
- 1/4 cup honey
- 1 whole vanilla bean, split lengthwise
- 1/4 teaspoon of salt (optional, but boosts the natural sweetness of the apples)

How to make it

1. First and foremost use a crockpot and the temperature should be set at high mode. Then put all the items and heat for five hours.
2. Before switching off the heat, take out the beans of vanilla and blend the applesauce till it becomes very smooth, and it's not lumpy.
3. Use a food processor or blender mixer to make it softer and to make an even finer blend.
4. You can apply the water bath method so that the sauce can be canned for later use, and the amount of sauce made from the above proportions would be four pints or half a gallon.

Tri Colored Potato Soup

- Serves 8-10 Servings

Ingredients

- 4 lbs Tri Colored Potato's (Gold, Purple, Red)
- 16 oz of Vegetable Stock
- 1 Small White Onion diced (approx. 1/2 cup)
- 3 – 4 Cloves Garlic
- 1 Tablespoon of Dill
- 2 teaspoons Sea Salt
- 1 teaspoon Ground Pepper
- 1 teaspoon Thyme
- 1 teaspoon Cayenne Pepper

How to make it:

1. Take the skin out of the potatoes and dice the potatoes.
2. Add some three or four garlic cloves and also put some chopped onions.
3. Now in a crock pot take all the items and add all the items and veggie broth.
4. The temperature should be set to high for around four hours and at low for around seven hours, these are for a slow cooker but when using a stovetop the numbers would change to three quarters of an hour when the setting is set at medium low.
5. The time isn't a factor, as you should cook it till the potatoes turn soft.

6. To embellish it you can use sour cream and chives, and also add some pureed soup.

Slow Cooker Split Pea Soup

- Prep time   10 mins
- Cook time 10 hours
- Total time 10 hours 10 mins
- Serves: 4 bowls

Ingredients

- 1¼ c. dried split peas, rinsed
- ½ small yellow onion (about ½ cup)
- 1 c. celery, chopped
- 2 carrots, chopped
- 2 garlic cloves, chopped
- 2 t. dried basil
- ½ t. dried rosemary
- 1 bay leaf
- 1 t. sea salt
- ½ t. black pepper
- 4 c. water
- 2 T. fresh parsley, chopped

How to make it

1. First put the items, which are mentioned in the list above in a sequential manner like starting with pea on the base of the pot and black pepper on top, add everything except the parsley.
2. Heat the soup at high setting for five to six hours and at low setting for nine to ten hours.
3. The soup should get thickened, if not then set the heat again back to high, and heat it till the excess water is soaked up.
4. Then use a spoon or dipper to pour it into soup bowls and embellish it with the parsley.
5. Your soup is ready to be savoured!

Easy Vegetable Soup

- Prep time : 10 mins
- Cook time : 40 mins
- Total time : 50 mins
- Serves: 8

Ingredients

- 1 onion, diced
- 1 head of celery, diced
- 1 lb bag of carrots, peeled and chopped - I only had a bag of baby carrots so I just used those and chopped them
- 6 red potatoes, cubed
- 1 pint grape tomatoes, halved

- 1 head of kale, chopped - I used an entire bag of Trader Joes Organic pre-washed and chopped kale
- 32 ounces chicken broth - I used my homemade bone broth, it's magical!
- 2 tsps garlic powder
- sea salt and fresh cracked pepper

How to make it

1. Take chicken broth, celery, onions, potatoes and carrots and put it in a crock pot while setting the crock pot at medium heat.
2. Fill the crock pot with water and put some cracked pepper, sea salt and some garlic powder in it.
3. The quantity of pepper and sea salt depends upon you, and heat the mix for about half an hour. Put the kale and tomatoes and blend it well.
4. Heat it for another ten minutes and can be served with toasted bread like Ezekiel.
5. With this you can savour it with a healthy soup, which also tastes good.

Braised Red Cabbage with Apples & Red Wine

- Yields: 4-6 portions
- Prep time: 15 mins
- Cook time: 50 min

Ingredients :-

- 1 Medium Head Red Cabbage, Finely Sliced
- 2 Apples, Cored And Cut Into Fine Stripes (Or Chopped)
- 1 Onion, Diced
- 3 Tablespoon Heat Stable Oil
- 8 Oz Vegetable Broth (Or Make Your Own! See Links Below)
- 3 Cloves
- 4 Tablespoon Red Wine Vinegar·
- 1 Cup Dry Red Wine·
- 1 Teaspoon Maple Syrup·
- 2 Bay Leaves·
- Salt, Pepper

How to make it

1. Take a big container or pot put some oil set the heat to medium.
2. Fry some onions and some apples in it for five minutes.
3. Put cabbage and fry for another five minutes.
4. Then pour all the items into it and put the cover on it and heat it for under an hour or fifty minutes.
5. You have to use a spoon to mix the items in between and when the cabbage becomes soft.
6. Add a hint of salt for flavour and it can be refrigerated for a maximum of seven days.

***********END *************

Conclusion

Thank you again for downloading this book!

I hope this book was able to give you the flavor that you have been looking for in your vitamin water.

The next step is to try the different recipes and share them with the people you hold dear.

Finally, if you enjoyed this book, please take the time to share your thoughts and post a review. It'd be greatly appreciated!

Thank you and good luck!

Did you enjoy this book?

I want to thank you for purchasing and reading this book. I really hope you got a lot out of it.

Can I ask a quick favor though?

If you enjoyed this book I would really appreciate it if you could leave me a positive review on Amazon.

I love getting feedback from my customers and reviews on Amazon really do make a difference. I read all my reviews and would really appreciate your thoughts.

If you have any questions, please feel free to mail me at beingpatriciabenson@yahoo.com

You can also LIKE My Facebook Page for updates and my upcoming book

Thanks so much.

Nancy Kelsey

Disclaimer

This Paleo Slow Cooker is written with an intention to serve as purely information and educational resource. It is not intended to be a medical advice or a medical guide.

Although proper care has been taken to ensure to validity and reliability of the information provided in this book. Readers are advice to exert caution before using any information, suggestion and methods described in this book.

The writer does not advocate the use of any of the suggestion, diet and health programs mention in this book. This book is not intended to take the place of a medical profession, a doctor and physician. The information in this book should not be used without the explicit advice from medically trained professions especially in cases where urgent diagnosis and medical treatment is needed.

The author or publisher cannot e held responsible for any personal or commercial damage in misinterpreting or misunderstanding any part of the book.

67204834R00061

Made in the USA
Lexington, KY
05 September 2017